IGNITE YOUR IMPACT

IGNITE YOUR IMPACT

A Blueprint for Launching Your Coaching Empire

GARY ROBBINS

Bald and Bonkers Network Academy

Contents

I

Introduction

The initial spark of interest in online coaching introduced me to a diverse array of individuals, many of whom were embarking on the journey of developing their own online coaching businesses. At first glance, it seemed like a promising community filled with like-minded enthusiasts. However, as I delved deeper into the digital realm, I discovered that a significant portion of these individuals was traversing a misguided path, armed with erroneous ideas on building and managing a successful online coaching enterprise.

To my detriment, I absorbed many of these misguided notions, leading to prolonged struggles in establishing my own coaching business. Among the perplexing and detrimental concepts I adopted was the belief that recruiting as many clients as possible for one-on-one coaching was the key to success. The rationale behind this seemed logical - having the coach physically present allows for real-time interaction, fostering a deeper understanding through immediate engagement and personalized inquiries.

While the advantages of face-to-face interaction are evident, the flaw in this logic lies in the assumption that people will actively seek one-on-one coaching unless the coach has already established themselves as a sought-after authority. The reality is that, as a coach, you must first prove your worth by paying your dues, authoring numerous books, participating in interviews, and building a recognizable presence in your industry.

However, this undertaking demands considerable effort, focus, and motivation, not to mention a significant investment of time. The ultimate goal is to cultivate a premium brand before promoting one-on-one coaching services, as potential clients are more inclined to invest in your expertise after recognizing your established reputation.

So, my advice is simple: invest in developing a premium brand first. While the journey may be challenging, some paths are more rewarding than others. It's essential to understand the qualities that set successful coaches apart and strive to incorporate them into your own practice.

When it comes to coaching, certain qualities consistently distinguish the most successful practitioners. Self-awareness is crucial, as a deep understanding of oneself is fundamental to effectively guiding others. Additionally, great communication, perceptiveness, professionalism, and flexibility are attributes that top coaches share. Developing these qualities will elevate your coaching practice and position you among the elite professionals making a positive impact.

In the realm of online coaching, the misconception that eloquence and a charismatic demeanor alone guarantee success is widespread. However, the reality is starkly different. Despite your perceived expertise, true success in online coaching requires more than just effective communication skills; it demands a strategic approach and a focus on specialization.

Becoming a successful coach involves far more than just presenting yourself as an expert. The road to real financial success in online coaching is intricate, demanding, and filled with challenges. It requires a strategic focus on specialization, as mere eloquence and social skills are insufficient to make a meaningful impact.

Rather than trying to be a jack-of-all-trades, concentrate on a niche that aligns with your expertise and delve deep into it. This focused approach will set you apart from the sea of generalists and establish you as a true authority in your field. Remember, the key is not just to know your subject matter but to comprehend it intimately and deliver tangible results that transform the lives of those seeking your guidance.

While many may be drawn to shortcuts, hype, and superficial branding, your commitment to doing the heavy lifting and genuinely communicating with your audience will make the critical difference. This resource serves as your guide to navigating the complexities of online coaching success. Build your business the right way from day one and set yourself on a trajectory toward lasting success.

To embark on the journey of online coaching success, it's crucial to recognize that the conventional belief in mere eloquence and surface-level branding as the key to prosperity is a myth. Achieving real success demands a profound understanding of the intricacies of your chosen field and a commitment to specialization.

While many may be enticed by the allure of quick wins, establishing a lasting coaching business requires a steadfast focus on specialization—an inch wide and miles deep. This involves not just acquiring knowledge but becoming a true master of your chosen domain. Your ability to articulate this expertise in clear terms and, most importantly, to deliver tangible results will elevate you from a mere practitioner to a trusted authority.

In a landscape where many are fixated on shortcuts, flashy branding, and networking tactics, your dedication to the arduous but rewarding path of specialization and genuine communication will set you apart. Avoid the trap of focusing solely on hype, superficial connections, and building a generic brand. The true differentiator lies in your willingness to do the heavy lifting and establish meaningful connections based on the value you bring to your audience.

This resource is more than a guide; it's a roadmap for building your online coaching business the right way from day one. Rather than succumbing to the allure of quick fixes, it encourages you to invest in the foundations of your expertise, ensuring that every step you take contributes to a sustainable and thriving coaching practice.

In conclusion, as you embark on the journey outlined in this guide, remember that success in online coaching is not just about the image you project or the charisma you exude—it's about becoming the real deal. Through specialization, diligent effort, and a genuine commitment to transforming the lives of those seeking your guidance, you'll not only stand out in a crowded market but also build a legacy of impact and success in the world of online coaching.

II

You Have To View Coaching
As A Business

Let's establish a fundamental truth: most people excel in at least one area of their lives. Whether driven by passion or the investment of time and energy into various activities, individuals tend to achieve expertise in specific domains. Indeed, each one of us can be considered an expert in at least one field.

However, the mistake many make is assuming that possessing expertise automatically translates into becoming a successful coach within that field. It's a common pitfall—individuals become enthralled with their knowledge and proudly proclaim themselves as the best local experts. While this self-confidence may be justified, problems arise when viewing coaching as a side pursuit rather than a serious venture.

This perspective is a disservice to oneself, setting the stage for potential failure. Merely being naturally adept at something does not guarantee the ability to deliver high-quality coaching services on one's own terms. While this approach might yield results in exceptional cases, for most individuals, it proves insufficient. Distractions, lack of focus, and confusion hinder the establishment of a solid brand offering a memorable service.

To truly succeed as an online coach, a mindset shift is essential—you must commit to and treat it as a genuine business. It's not just a sideline activity; it's a venture that demands a strategic approach. Success comes from systematically addressing challenges, solving them one by one, and making the necessary hard decisions.

Unfortunately, many aspiring online coaches fall into the trap of focusing solely on their passion and the number of people they can help with their expertise. While these are commendable aspects, they fall short unless viewed within the broader context of a business. Without this perspective, prolonged struggles and unmet financial expectations may persist.

Running an online coaching business demands treating it as a business from the outset, making informed decisions, and establishing systematic, methodical processes. This guide provides invaluable insights into the often complex and confusing process of building a successful online coaching business—a resource that, while not suitable for everyone, significantly enhances the chances of success for those with the right plan.

Moving forward, it's crucial to recognize that your most precious coaching asset is your personal brand. Many online coaching business owners possess extensive knowledge and expertise developed over years of passionate curiosity in their respective fields. While raw knowledge and the desire to help are crucial, they alone do not guarantee success in the coaching business. There's a missing piece—an element beyond expertise and passion.

Becoming an expert and knowing your stuff is only a fraction of the broader picture. Regardless of competence and experience, the majority of your activities as an online coach must focus on building your personal brand. While expertise establishes credibility, marketing yourself is equally crucial. Having a stellar product or service is one thing; ensuring enough people are aware of it is another.

It's not enough to think that the selling process is beneath you. Passion for your expertise should translate into a willingness to share it with the world. Recognize that there are numerous experts in the same arena, all vying for attention and clients. To stand out, you must actively find ways to get noticed.

If you keep your knowledge to yourself or provide inconsistent coaching services, you are hindering your progress. Building a solid brand is the key—a factor that distinguishes businesses like McDonald's from local burger stands. Regardless of personal opinions on food quality, McDonald's is recognized globally due to its solid brand.

Contrary to common misconceptions, developing a solid brand doesn't require exorbitant spending or extensive connections. Instead, it demands knowledge of the right methods and a systematic, methodical plan. The failure of many in building a personal brand often results from a lack of such a plan. The guide offers a structured approach to avoid the pitfalls and guide you in establishing a brand that sets you apart in the competitive landscape of online coaching.

Building a brand that resonates and stands out doesn't have to be a complex or overwhelming process. In fact, with the right approach, anyone can develop a strong personal brand. It's not just about having the expertise; it's about strategically showcasing that expertise to the world.

Consider the comparison between corner

burger stands and global brands like McDonald's. Regardless of individual opinions about the quality of food, there's no denying the power of McDonald's as a global brand. This recognition is a result of a carefully crafted and consistently communicated brand identity. Similarly, as an online coach, you have the opportunity to establish a brand that speaks to your unique strengths and resonates with your target audience.

Believe it or not, developing a solid brand is a step-by-step process that doesn't require a substantial financial investment or a vast network of connections. What it does demand is a systematic and methodical plan, and this is precisely what this guide aims to provide.

Many people stumble in building a personal brand not because they lack passion or expertise but because they lack a structured approach. This guide breaks down the process, offering insights into the right sequence of steps to take. By following a systematic plan, you can avoid common pitfalls, leverage your strengths, and establish a brand that not only showcases your expertise but also captivates your audience.

The journey to success as an online coach involves more than just knowing your stuff; it requires an understanding of the business side of coaching. Treating your coaching practice as a business means embracing the challenges, making strategic decisions, and committing to a continuous process of improvement.

In essence, this guide is your companion in navigating the intricacies of the coaching business. It's a valuable resource that goes beyond theoretical knowledge, providing actionable steps and insights to help you build a thriving online coaching business. Remember, success in this field is not just about what you know; it's about how effectively you can communicate and market your expertise to the world.

By internalizing the principles outlined in this guide, you'll be well-equipped to overcome challenges, set up your coaching practice in a systematic manner, and increase your chances of achieving the success you envision. Don't waste precious time trying to figure things out the hard way—embrace the guidance offered here, commit to the process, and position yourself for lasting success in the world of online coaching. Your journey to building a successful coaching business starts now.

As you embark on the journey outlined in this guide, consider it not just as a manual but as a roadmap tailored to your unique path in the world of online coaching. Success in this field requires more than a mere accumulation of knowledge or a passion for a particular subject; it demands a strategic mindset and a commitment to viewing your coaching endeavors as a bona fide business.

The misconception that knowing your subject matter is sufficient for success is a common pitfall. While expertise is undoubtedly crucial, it forms only a small fraction of the larger picture. Your activities as an online coach, regardless of your competence and experience, must extend beyond your proficiency in the subject. This guide emphasizes the importance of treating your coaching practice as a business from the outset—a perspective that sets the stage for resilience, growth, and sustainable success.

The notion of a "business mindset" involves acknowledging and addressing difficulties head-on. It means unraveling challenges systematically, making informed decisions, and navigating the entrepreneurial landscape with purpose and focus. Too often, aspiring online coaches miss this crucial point, remaining fixated on their passion without realizing that a strategic approach is necessary to transform that passion into a lucrative venture.

Passion alone won't sustain your coaching business; you must integrate it into a well-organized, methodical structure. This guide offers you access to information that will guide you through the often intricate process of establishing a successful online coaching business. While it might not be suitable for everyone, if you have the right plan, it significantly enhances your chances of success.

Moving forward, recognize that your personal brand is your most valuable asset. Even if you possess extensive knowledge and expertise, a lack of strategic branding can impede your success as an online coach. Understanding your subject matter is the first step, but marketing yourself is equally crucial. This guide encourages you to embrace the selling process, as reluctance in this aspect often leads to prolonged struggles.

Standing out in a crowded field of online coaches requires more than just knowing your stuff; it demands building a brand that captivates and resonates. A solid brand distinguishes you from the myriad other experts, much like how McDonald's stands apart from local burger stands. Developing such a brand doesn't necessitate exorbitant spending or extensive connections but does require a systematic and methodical plan—a plan that this guide helps you formulate.

Remember, success in online coaching is not just about your knowledge; it's about how effectively you communicate and market that knowledge. By diligently following the principles outlined in this guide, you position yourself to overcome challenges, establish your coaching practice systematically, and increase your likelihood of achieving the success you aspire to.

Your journey in the world of online coaching is unique, and this guide is designed to be your companion, providing insights, strategies, and practical steps to guide you toward success. Embrace this resource, commit to the process, and lay the foundation for a lasting and prosperous coaching business. The path to success as an online coach unfolds one step at a time, and with the right guidance, you're well on your way to realizing your goals. Best of luck on your journey!

III

Coaches Need To Constantly Challenge Their Knowledge

When delving into the realm of life coaching, the digital landscape is inundated with individuals claiming to be professionals in this field. The allure of starting a life coaching practice, coupled with the relatively low startup costs and minimal training requirements, has led to a surge in people joining the bandwagon of life coaching. This influx is partly fueled by popular programs that portray life coaching as an accessible and straightforward endeavor.

However, amidst this influx of aspiring life coaches, distinguishing the professionals from the amateurs becomes crucial. Here are five signs that can serve as indicators of whether a life coach is a professional:

1. *Professional Website Presence:*

Professionals in the field typically boast a well-designed and organized website. While those starting out might resort to cost-saving measures, professionals invest in a professional online presence, setting them apart from newcomers.

2. *Organized and Detail-Oriented:*

A hallmark of a good coach is their meticulous note-taking and organizational skills. Professionals are adept at keeping track of information, ensuring easy retrieval when needed. Their attention to detail sets them apart in delivering quality coaching services.

3. *Demonstrable Success Through Referrals:*

A reliable measure of a coach's competence is their ability to showcase satisfied clients who willingly refer others. If a coach hesitates or cannot provide referrals, despite having been in business for a while, it raises questions about their professionalism.

4. Financial Stability and Selectivity:

Professionals in the coaching industry manage their finances effectively. Unlike amateurs who may resort to drastic measures to attract clients, professionals maintain a level of financial comfort. They can afford to be selective with their clientele, a testament to their expertise and demand.

5. Positive, Punctual, and Prepared:

The three P's—positivity, punctuality, and preparedness—are integral to professional coaching. Successful coaches exude a positive attitude, remain punctual, and arrive prepared for every session with notes, tools, and necessary paperwork.

Mistakes to Avoid When Coaching Online:

If venturing into online coaching, it's crucial to hone your skills before taking on clients. While making mistakes is an inevitable part of any new endeavor, avoiding certain pitfalls can prevent detrimental consequences to your budding coaching business. Here are four mistakes to steer clear of:

1. Overcommitting:

Attempting to do everything often results in accomplishing very little. Focusing on a few aspects and excelling in them is more productive than spreading yourself too thin across various roles and responsibilities.

2. *Neglecting Website Quality:*

A poorly designed website reflects negatively on your brand. Investing time and resources in creating an appealing, professional website is essential, as it serves as the face of your online presence.

3. *Excessive Focus on Training and Certification:*

While training is crucial, excessive emphasis on certifications at the expense of other business aspects can hinder your ability to attract clients. Strike a balance between acquiring essential training and investing in the growth and promotion of your coaching business.

4. *Insufficient Financial Preparedness:*

Starting a coaching business without a financial cushion can hinder its growth. Allocate funds not only for initial business investments but also for ongoing promotions and sustaining yourself if you decide to pursue coaching full-time.

In essence, navigating the realm of life coaching demands a discerning eye to distinguish between professionals and enthusiasts. Additionally, avoiding common pitfalls in the online coaching sphere sets the foundation for a successful and sustainable coaching business. The path to success involves not only learning from mistakes but also making informed decisions and strategic investments.

Building a Robust Online Coaching Practice:

To truly excel in the realm of online coaching, aspiring coaches must recognize that success is a journey of continuous learning, strategic planning, and adept decision-making. Here's a more detailed exploration of key elements to consider as you embark on this transformative path:

1. Strategic Focus:

Instead of trying to do everything, focus on a select few areas where your strengths lie. Whether you're a writer, a coach, a content creator, or an entrepreneur, honing in on specific skills allows you to deliver quality in your chosen domains.

2. Investing in Website Excellence:

Your website is the digital face of your coaching business. While cost-saving measures might be tempting, allocating time and resources to create an exceptional website is an investment in your brand's perception. A professional-looking site enhances credibility and attracts potential clients.

3. Balancing Training and Business Investment:

While continuous learning is essential, striking a balance between acquiring necessary training and investing in your business infrastructure is crucial. Prioritize investments in tools, equipment, and promotional efforts alongside acquiring the knowledge needed to excel in your coaching practice.

4. Financial Preparedness:

Building a financial cushion is indispensable for the longevity of your coaching business. Allocate funds not only for the initial setup but also for ongoing marketing efforts, professional development, and sustaining yourself if you decide to transition to full-time coaching.

5. Client-Focused Approach:

A professional coach places the needs of their clients at the forefront. Demonstrating success through client referrals is a powerful testament to your coaching prowess. Establishing a track record of satisfied clients who willingly recommend your services is a sign of professionalism and competence.

6. Embracing Positivity, Punctuality, and Preparedness:

The three P's—positivity, punctuality, and preparedness—serve as the foundation for a professional coaching practice. Maintaining a positive attitude, respecting clients' time through punctuality, and arriving prepared for each session are hallmarks of a seasoned and reliable coach.

Conclusion:

Embarking on a career in online coaching is a journey filled with opportunities for growth and success. By heeding the signs of professionalism, avoiding common pitfalls, and adopting a strategic mindset, you position yourself for long-term success in the ever-evolving landscape of coaching.

Remember that success is not just about what you know but how effectively you apply that knowledge to connect with and assist your clients.

Continuously learn, adapt, and refine your approach, and you'll find yourself not only building a successful coaching business but making a meaningful impact in the lives of those you serve.

This comprehensive guide serves as a valuable companion on your journey, offering insights, strategies, and practical advice to navigate the complexities of online coaching. Embrace the opportunities, learn from experiences, and with the right mindset, you're well on your way to establishing a thriving and fulfilling online coaching practice. Wishing you continued success and fulfillment in your coaching endeavors!

IV

Finding the Root Cause of Your Client's Obstacles

Unraveling the Roots: A Deeper Look into Coaching Dynamics

In the intricate landscape of coaching, sometimes the surface issues are mere manifestations of deeper-rooted concerns. Understanding the belief-thought-action cycle becomes paramount in unraveling the complexities of human behavior during sporadic coaching sessions.

Believing, Thinking & Acting: The Core Cycle

The belief-thought-action cycle is a continuous process that shapes our behaviors. Delving into this cycle allows coaches to identify the driving beliefs behind destructive actions. Actions, seemingly spontaneous, are often predetermined by the thoughts influenced by underlying beliefs.

Actions:

While actions may appear to be conscious choices, they are, in reality, predetermined by our thoughts. Examining recurring behaviors, such as a client's hesitation to engage with the opposite sex, necessitates an exploration of the underlying thoughts.

Thoughts:

Thoughts are the driving force behind actions. For instance, a client may believe they lack the ability to communicate effectively, leading to thoughts of inadequacy that drive their actions.

Beliefs:

Tracing behaviors back to their origin often unveils deep-seated beliefs. In the example, the belief may be rooted in a sense of inadequacy, leading to a fear of engaging with attractive individuals of the opposite sex.

Guiding clients through this introspective journey enables them to evaluate and potentially alter limiting beliefs, paving the way for positive behavioral change.

Navigating Difficult Clients: A Strategic Approach

In the coaching realm, encounters with challenging clients are inevitable. Recognizing and effectively managing these "problem clients" requires a proactive strategy.

Commitment Without Over-Investment: While commitment to a client's success is essential, maintaining emotional distance is crucial. Over-investment in a client's success may lead to personal disappointment if expectations aren't met.

Identifying Warning Signs: Vigilance for warning signs is a skill acquired through experience. Early identification of potential issues allows coaches to address concerns before they escalate.

Energy Management: If a client consistently drains your energy or leaves you feeling negatively impacted, consider the possibility of parting ways.

Preserving your well-being ensures optimal support for other clients.

Open Communication: Establish clear ground rules and maintain open communication. Addressing issues directly and expressing concerns ensures a healthy coaching relationship.

Overcoming the Fear of Failure: Strategies for New Coaches

Embarking on a coaching journey can evoke doubt and fear. Overcoming the fear of failure requires a combination of practical steps and a mindset shift.

Offer Free Sessions: Begin by offering free sessions to gain valuable experience without the pressure of payment. This approach allows you to refine your coaching skills with genuine feedback.

Start with Short Sessions: Initiate coaching with shorter sessions, providing a manageable entry point. This not only reduces the perceived pressure but also builds your confidence gradually.

Practice with Familiar Faces: Utilize friends or family members as initial clients to practice coaching in a familiar environment. This familiarity alleviates the anxiety associated with coaching strangers.

Remind Yourself of Your Purpose: Regularly revisit the reasons behind your decision to become a coach. Reaffirm your belief in the value you bring to your clients, and trust that your chosen path is driven by a genuine desire to make a positive impact.

Navigating the Coaching Landscape

Coaching, with its intricacies and challenges, is a dynamic journey of continuous learning and growth. By understanding the underlying dynamics of human behavior, strategically managing difficult client interactions, and overcoming the fear of failure, you position yourself for sustained success in the coaching realm.

Remember, every coach encounters moments of doubt, but it is through experience, resilience, and a commitment to personal and professional growth that you emerge as a confident and impactful coach. Embrace the journey, learn from each experience, and watch as your coaching practice flourishes into a beacon of positive change for those you serve.

Elevating Coaching Proficiency: A Journey of Continuous Improvement

As you navigate the complexities of coaching, consider professional development as an ongoing process. Mastery in coaching involves a commitment to continuous improvement, staying abreast of industry trends, and refining your skills.

Engage in Advanced Training: Pursue advanced training courses to deepen your understanding of coaching methodologies, behavioral psychology, and effective communication strategies. This investment enhances your expertise and allows you to offer diverse and comprehensive coaching services.

Seek Mentorship: Collaborate with experienced mentors in the coaching field. Their guidance provides invaluable insights, helping you navigate challenges, refine your coaching approach, and gain a broader perspective on the profession.

Stay Informed About Industry Trends: The coaching landscape is dynamic, with emerging trends shaping client expectations. Regularly update your knowledge about industry trends, technological advancements, and evolving coaching methodologies to ensure relevance and effectiveness in your practice.

Embrace Feedback and Self-Reflection: Foster a culture of continuous improvement by actively seeking feedback from clients, peers, and mentors. Embrace constructive criticism as a catalyst for growth and refine your coaching techniques through regular self-reflection.

Expanding Your Reach: Building a Strong Online Presence

In the digital age, establishing a robust online presence is essential for expanding your reach and attracting potential clients. Leverage various platforms to showcase your expertise, connect with your audience, and establish yourself as a reputable coach.

Create a Professional Website: A well-designed website serves as your virtual storefront. Ensure it reflects your coaching philosophy, showcases client success stories, and provides clear information about your services. Optimize it for search engines to enhance visibility.

Utilize Social Media: Engage with a broader audience by leveraging social media platforms. Share valuable content, participate in relevant conversations, and demonstrate your expertise. Building a strong online community can lead to client referrals and increased visibility.

Start a Blog or Podcast: Establish yourself as a thought leader by creating a blog or podcast. Share insights, discuss relevant topics, and offer practical advice. Consistent content creation enhances your credibility and attracts individuals seeking your expertise.

Network Effectively: Join online coaching communities, participate in forums, and attend virtual events to network with peers and potential clients. Building a strong online network fosters collaboration, provides learning opportunities, and expands your professional connections.

Thriving Amidst Challenges: The Coach's Resilient Spirit

In challenging economic times, maintaining

financial stability as a coach requires strategic planning and adaptability.

Diversify Your Services: Explore diverse coaching services or create specialized programs to cater to a broader client base. Offering workshops, webinars, or group coaching sessions can complement individual coaching services.

Adjust Pricing Strategically: Evaluate your pricing strategy based on market trends, your expertise, and the value you provide. Consider offering flexible payment plans or packages to accommodate varying client budgets.

Build Resilience Through Savings: Establish a financial safety net by consistently saving a portion of your earnings. This reserve can serve as a buffer during lean periods and provide peace of mind as you navigate economic fluctuations.

Embracing Technological Advancements: Enhancing Coaching Efficiency

Incorporating technological advancements into your coaching practice can enhance efficiency, improve client experiences, and streamline administrative tasks.

Explore Virtual Coaching Platforms: Embrace virtual coaching platforms that offer secure and user-friendly interfaces. Video conferencing, messaging, and file-sharing functionalities can facilitate seamless communication with clients.

Implement Client Management Software: Invest in client management software to organize schedules, track client progress, and streamline administrative tasks. Automation can enhance efficiency, allowing you to focus more on coaching.

Stay Informed About Industry Tools: Regularly explore emerging tools and technologies within the coaching industry. From assessment tools to interactive platforms, staying informed ensures you leverage innovations to benefit both you and your clients.

In Conclusion: A Flourishing Coaching Journey

Embarking on a coaching journey is a dynamic and transformative experience. As you navigate the intricacies of coaching, continuously prioritize your professional development, embrace digital advancements, and maintain resilience in the face of challenges.

Remember, each challenge presents an opportunity for growth, and your commitment to evolving as a coach will propel your practice to new heights. Stay passionate, stay informed, and relish the profound impact you have on the lives of those you guide toward positive transformation. The coaching journey is not just a profession; it's a continuous odyssey of learning, adapting, and thriving.

V

❧

Reasons Life and Business Coaches Fail

BUILDING A SUCCESSFUL COACHING CAREER: NAVIGATING CHALLENGES AND SETTING THE FOUNDATION

Embarking on the Coaching Journey: A Thrilling Pursuit

Entering the world of life or business coaching is a commendable goal, offering the potential for personal fulfillment and significant impact on others. While many achieve remarkable success, it's crucial to acknowledge the challenges and pitfalls that others have faced on this journey. Understanding these obstacles equips you with the knowledge to navigate them successfully.

RECOGNIZING THE ODDS: SUCCESS AMIDST CHALLENGES

The coaching industry is undoubtedly rewarding, but it's essential to recognize that not everyone attains the same level of success. For every coach who breaks into the industry, builds a devoted following, and earns a sustainable income, there are fifteen others who face challenges. This isn't meant to discourage you but to emphasize the importance of being informed and prepared.

Top Reasons Coaches Encounter Failure: Insights and Solutions

Let's delve into some common reasons coaches face setbacks and explore strategies to avoid these pitfalls:

1. Being Too Formulaic:

- *Challenge:* Using a one-size-fits-all approach limits success.

- *Solution:* Embrace flexibility and adapt your methods to cater to the unique needs of each client. A personalized approach enhances effectiveness.

2. Lacking Confidence:

- *Challenge:* Insecurity undermines the coach-client relationship.

- *Solution:* Prioritize self-development and affirm your capabilities daily. Confidence in yourself translates to confidence from your clients.

3. Copying Others:

- *Challenge:* Imitating others stifles your potential as a leader.

- *Solution:* Learn from mentors but forge your unique coaching style. True leaders innovate and create their path.

4. Lack of Persistence:

- *Challenge:* Impatience and a lack of persistence impede long-term success.

- *Solution:* Persevere through challenges, understanding that building a clientele and a thriving coaching practice takes time.

Certification and Training: Navigating the Landscape

Entering the coaching arena often prompts questions about training and certification. While there's no mandatory regulatory body, legitimate certifications enhance credibility and open doors. However, not all certifications carry the same weight.

Choosing Legitimate Training and Certification: Strategies for Success

To navigate the myriad of training programs and certifications, consider the following strategies:

1. *Seek Recommendations:*
- *Approach:* Explore coaching forums where experienced coaches share insights.
- *Benefit:* Learn about reputable programs through peer recommendations, ensuring your training holds value in the coaching community.

2. Consider Brand Reputation:

- *Approach:* Opt for certifications associated with respected figures like Tony Robbins.

- *Benefit:* A well-known brand adds credibility to your certification, enhancing your standing among clients and fellow coaches.

Top Training Programs for Aspiring Coaches: A Roadmap to Excellence

Institute for Professionalism Excellence in Coaching (iPEC):

- *Overview:* An accredited coaching program with diverse coaching tracks.

- *Benefits:* iPEC's reputation and extensive training programs make it a respected choice.

International Coach Federation (ICF):

- *Overview:* A non-profit accrediting agency providing recommendations on reputable programs.

- *Benefits:* ICF-approved programs ensure adherence to industry standards, recognized globally.

Ericson International:

- *Overview:* An accredited training school offering comprehensive coaching training.

- *Benefits:* Known for turning out exceptional coaches, Ericson's online training provides accessibility and flexibility.

Robbins-Madanes Training:

- *Overview:* Founded by Tony Robbins, Mark and Magali Peysha, and therapist Cloe Madanes.

- *Benefits:* Board certification, respected Core 100 and Core 200 training, and Breakthrough Training contribute to its esteemed reputation.

Conclusion: A Journey of Growth and Impact

Embarking on a coaching career is not just a professional endeavor but a transformative journey of growth and impact. Acknowledge the challenges, equip yourself with relevant skills, and leverage reputable training programs to ensure a fulfilling and successful coaching practice. Your commitment to continuous learning, adaptability, and authenticity will set the foundation for a flourishing coaching career. Embrace the odyssey

ahead, and may it be marked by profound positive transformations for both yourself and those
you guide.

VI

Successful Online Coaches Need To Work The Media

MASTERING MEDIA ENGAGEMENT FOR COACHING SUCCESS: A STRATEGIC APPROACH

Understanding the Essence: Working the Media, Not Working for It

Take a moment to reflect on the title of this article. Can you reiterate it? Excellent. It's crucial to highlight that the emphasis is on successful coaches working the media, not working for it.

This distinction holds significant importance, often misunderstood by many aspiring coaches.

A common misconception prevails among individuals attempting to gain traction in their online coaching ventures – the belief that working for the media, producing endless content in hopes of media recognition, is the key to success. Unfortunately, this approach is flawed and unlikely to yield the desired results.

The Pitfall of Playing the Waiting Game

Hoping that media exposure alone will elevate your brand to the desired heights is a risky strategy. Merely assuming that media attention will magically transform your brand is a passive approach that often leads to disappointment. To truly succeed, you must actively engage and work the media.

Playing the Media Game Strategically

In the age of social media and continuous news cycles, a more direct involvement is required. The key is to work the media instead of working for it. Discard the notion of churning out content blindly and hoping for media recognition. Instead, adopt a proactive role in shaping your brand's narrative.

Strategies for Effective Media Engagement

1. Utilizing Online Resources:

- Engage with platforms like Help a Reporter Out (HARO) to position yourself as an expert.

- Provide your area of expertise, allowing journalists and reporters to connect with you when seeking knowledgeable sources.

2. Crafting Newsworthy Press Releases:

- Develop press releases that align with controversial topics within your industry.

- Demonstrate imagination, resourcefulness, and creativity to present your brand within a compelling narrative.

Navigating the Challenges of Online Coaching Success

Building a successful online coaching business

requires a multifaceted approach. Playing the media game strategically is just one aspect. It involves utilizing various tools, such as HARO, and crafting press releases that capture attention within your industry.

Social Media: A Non-Negotiable Asset for Coaching Success

Dispelling the myth of a division between online and offline businesses, social media emerges as an indispensable tool for all. Regardless of your business's nature – entirely online, offline, or a blend of both – social media is not merely an option but an absolute necessity.

Understanding the Power of Social Media Exposure

The potency of social media exposure cannot be overstated. Even with a modest following, the viral nature of social media can catapult your brand to unexpected heights. Each follower you gain has the potential to expand your reach exponentially, leading to millions of impressions.

The Exponential Impact of Social Media: A Viral Chain Reaction

A small following can trigger a chain reaction of sharing and resharing. This cascading effect among circles of influence can result in exponential growth. Your initial 500 followers could potentially translate into reaching millions, contingent upon the appeal of your content.

A Cautionary Tale: Neglecting Social Media Can Be Detrimental

Delaying the implementation of a responsive and strategic social media plan may jeopardize your business's future. Businesses that underestimate the significance of social media, considering it an afterthought, often face regrettable consequences.

The Imperative of Visibility: A Call to Action

Establishing a visible online presence is not rocket science. Create platforms on YouTube, Twitter, and Facebook, ensuring consistent messaging with your coaching business website. Visibility across these platforms forms a critical component of playing the game the right way.

Conclusion: A Proactive Approach to Coaching Success

In the dynamic landscape of coaching, success demands an active role in media engagement and an unwavering commitment to social media visibility. By working the media strategically and recognizing the indispensable role of social media, you pave the way for sustained success in your coaching business. Embrace these strategies, stay proactive, and witness the transformative impact on your coaching journey.

VII

Enhance Your Market Value Through Controversy

In the ever-evolving landscape of your industry, the ability to confront controversies head-on emerges as one of the most potent strategies to position yourself as a recognized expert. Rather than shying away from controversial positions and avoiding potential disagreement, seizing the opportunity to engage with controversy can propel your expertise to new heights.

Regardless of how niche, harmless, or esoteric

your specific industry may be, disagreements are inherent. This is a natural outcome of engaging with a diverse audience comprised of individuals with varying perspectives. Understanding this diversity is crucial, for in any human interaction, there exists the potential for contrasting viewpoints.

The presence of controversy is not a negative aspect to be avoided; it is, in fact, a canvas of endless possibilities and opportunities for both small and significant disagreements. Controversy, as a perpetual companion in your professional journey, offers chances for growth, learning, and, most importantly, a platform to showcase your expertise.

Every controversy is an opportunity for you to articulate your unique insights and demonstrate why you are an authority in your field. It's not about imposing your views on others; rather, it's an invitation to engage in informed discussions. When you embrace this opportunity, you broadcast to your audience that you possess a profound understanding of your industry.

Engaging in respectful, fact-driven, and results-oriented debates on controversial topics within your industry showcases your commitment to being on top of your game. While others may choose to evade such discussions, you stand out as a courageous voice willing to confront challenges directly. This courage adds a significant layer to your professional image, making you look not just competent but also bold and authoritative.

By not succumbing to the temptation of avoiding controversies and taking a stand instead, you distinguish yourself from the crowd of self-proclaimed experts. While others might be scrambling to evade confrontation, you position yourself as one of the few voices in your industry unafraid to tackle controversial issues head-on.

This approach not only makes you look good but also elevates your brand image. You become a symbol of resilience and confidence, turning potential points of division or disagreement into opportunities for growth and professional development. Speaking up and letting your voice be heard amid controversies becomes a powerful strategy to promote your expertise, and you might find that your brand gains even more recognition as a result of your willingness to stand up to challenges.

Group Coaching

Group coaching programs have surged in popularity due to their unique ability to allow coaches to serve a larger clientele in a more time-efficient manner. The introduction of the private group feature on platforms like Facebook has particularly contributed to the widespread adoption of this coaching approach. Unlike traditional one-on-one coaching, group coaching involves bringing discussions into a smaller, more intimate space, fostering conversations that delve into topics such as goal setting, taking action, and accountability.

The growing appeal of group coaching can be attributed to the sense of community it offers, which is often lacking in traditional one-on-one programs. The dynamics of a group setting, facilitated by forums or dedicated Facebook groups, enable members to interact, support each other, seek guidance, and form meaningful relationships. This community-oriented approach provides a robust support system, offering a shoulder to lean on during challenging times and a chorus of supporters to celebrate achievements and milestones.

While one-on-one coaching places the spotlight solely on the individual and their progress, group coaching introduces a more diversified and collaborative approach. The varied perspectives within a group contribute to a richer learning environment, and the sense of camaraderie becomes a powerful motivator.

Affordability is another key advantage of group coaching programs. Not everyone may be ready or able to invest in private coaching sessions, making group programs an attractive and accessible option. The lower cost serves as a lead-in for individuals who may later transition to higher-priced programs as they gain confidence in the value they receive.

One major advantage of group coaching is its flexibility and convenience for both coaches and clients. The asynchronous nature of group interactions allows participants to engage at their own pace, contributing to discussions and seeking support whenever it fits into their schedules. This flexibility accommodates the diverse commitments and responsibilities of both coaches and clients.

Platforms like Facebook provide additional advantages for group coaching. The subscription-based model, for instance, allows coaches to monetize their groups effectively. With features like post scheduling, live broadcasting, and multimedia sharing, coaches can create a dynamic and engaging environment for their members.

Utilizing Facebook advertising further enhances the reach of group coaching programs. By running targeted ad campaigns or boosting posts, coaches can connect with their ideal audience cost-effectively, ensuring a steady influx of new members.

When it comes to attracting members, simplicity is key. Clear calls to action, noticeable "buy" buttons, and easy navigation are crucial elements on sales pages. Email marketing proves to be an effective strategy for enticing potential members. Building and leveraging an email list allows coaches to provide updates, share insights about group activities, and offer special promotions, creating anticipation and eagerness among potential members.

In summary, group coaching programs offer a holistic and community-driven approach to personal and professional development, making them an increasingly preferred choice for both coaches and clients alike. The combination of affordability, convenience, and community support positions group coaching as a versatile and effective coaching model.

IX

Host a Successful Group Coaching Program

Creating a successful group coaching program requires careful planning and effective marketing strategies to attract individuals interested in your services. A well-structured marketing funnel is essential for this purpose, encompassing various elements:

1. Website:

- Establish a professional website that serves as the cornerstone of your online presence.

- Ensure an attractive design that aligns with your brand image.

2. Compelling Sales Copy:

- Craft persuasive and compelling sales copy that clearly communicates the value of your coaching program.

- Clearly articulate the benefits of joining your group and what sets it apart.

3. Email Collection:

- Implement a reliable email marketing platform like Aweber or Getresponse to collect email addresses.

- Offer incentives, such as free reports or training, to encourage visitors to join your email list.

4. Call to Action (CTA):

- Create a solid call to action (CTA) on your website with a prominently placed buy button.

- Guide visitors seamlessly through the process of expressing interest in your coaching program.

Once these foundational elements are in place, the focus shifts to the pivotal aspect of marketing, an area that often poses challenges for many coaches aiming for success. Overcoming barriers like uncertainty about where to start, fear of self-promotion, or underestimating the importance of marketing is crucial. Without effective promotion, it's challenging to attract the audience needed to fill your group.

Even with limited marketing experience, coaches can employ proven strategies to promote their group successfully. Here are some ideas to kickstart your marketing efforts:

1. Build Your Public Profile:

- Leverage your website as a platform to create and promote your public image or brand.

- Consider your website as an interactive billboard, shaping the perception you want the world to have.

2. Utilize Social Proof:

- Incorporate testimonials from satisfied customers to build trust.

- Ratings and reviews serve as additional tools to influence potential clients positively.

3. Paid Traffic (Facebook Ads):

- Utilize Facebook ads, a cost-effective method with extensive reach and targeted marketing capabilities.

- Leverage the retargeting pixel to reconnect

with individuals who have engaged with your website or joined your email list.

4. Host a Webinar:

- Conduct live webinars to showcase your personality, skills, and knowledge.

- Use webinars as a platform to share valuable information, establishing yourself as an authority in your niche.

Promoting your coaching program doesn't require an advanced marketing degree. Starting with fundamental strategies and gradually expanding your efforts will contribute to positioning your group for success. Building a public profile, incorporating social proof, leveraging paid traffic through platforms like Facebook, and hosting webinars are effective ways to increase visibility and attract potential clients.

To further enhance your coaching program's success, consider the importance of constructing a well-designed marketing funnel. A properly configured funnel can lead to a predictable and steady flow of potential clients. The top of the funnel focuses on creating awareness and educating consumers about your coaching group. This phase aims to entice them to take action, such as joining your email list.

Moving down the funnel, low-cost offers, or "tripwires," provide an opportunity for consumers to engage with your coaching style without a significant financial commitment. This could involve ebooks, short reports, or self-study courses. The mid and high-priced offers, including your group coaching program, come next, requiring a higher level of commitment but offering a perceived higher value.

Consider offering different levels within your group coaching program to cater to varied needs and preferences. For example, entry-level access, mid-level interaction, and high-level direct consultation can accommodate diverse client requirements.

A well-structured coaching funnel might progress from free webinars to low-cost and mid-cost group coaching before reaching high-end private coaching. While not all clients will traverse the entire funnel, building it with the expectation of such progression allows for flexibility and adjustments.

In summary, mastering the art of promotion and constructing an effective coaching funnel are key elements in hosting a successful group coaching program. Starting with the basics and gradually expanding your strategies will contribute to the growth and sustainability of your coaching business.

X

Final Words

As a dedicated life coach, witnessing the success of your clients is not just a professional achievement; it's a source of immense personal satisfaction. The profound joy derived from seeing your clients accomplish the goals they set for themselves transcends mere professional fulfillment. Not only does their success validate your coaching expertise, but it also becomes a powerful motivator for your future engagements with other clients.

The benefits extend beyond personal gratification. When a client triumphs under your guidance, it not only strengthens your professional reputation but also opens avenues for future collaborations. Impressing a client with your coaching prowess often leads to repeat business, as they return for further guidance on new endeavors. Furthermore, satisfied clients become your brand ambassadors, sharing their success stories with friends and family, thereby enhancing your credibility and attracting a broader clientele.

To maximize your clients' chances of success, consider incorporating three powerful strategies into your coaching approach:

1. *Commitment to Success:*

Ensure that your clients are not merely pursuing goals half-heartedly but are genuinely committed to making them a reality. True commitment involves a willingness to invest effort, sacrifice time, and overcome challenges. Clients who understand the costs and are prepared to make the necessary sacrifices become nearly unstoppable forces on their path to success.

2. *Risk Awareness and Willingness:*

Every worthwhile goal involves inherent risks. It's essential to assess whether your clients are fully aware of the risks associated with their goals and, more importantly, if they are willing to face and overcome these challenges. Whether it's investing time, money, or other resources, clients who comprehend the risks and still proceed demonstrate a resilience that significantly enhances their chances of success.

3. *Passionate Pursuit of Goals:*

Assess the depth of your client's passion for their chosen goals. Successful individuals are often characterized by an unwavering passion for what they do. The sheer joy and enthusiasm they derive from pursuing their objectives transform the journey into a pleasurable experience rather than a burdensome task. Encourage your clients to cultivate a profound love for their goals, as this passion becomes a driving force propelling them towards success.

Incorporating these strategies into your coaching methodology ensures that you are not only imparting valuable guidance but also creating a framework for your clients' success. By instilling commitment, addressing risks, and fostering passion, you contribute significantly to enhancing their likelihood of reaching and surpassing their goals. Ultimately, your role as a life coach becomes a transformative force, empowering individuals to unlock their full potential and achieve remarkable success.

Moreover, to amplify the impact of your coaching, consider weaving these strategies into the fabric of your coaching sessions:

1. *Establishing Commitment:*

Begin by engaging your clients in deep conversations about their commitment levels. Explore the extent to which they are willing to invest their time, energy, and resources to achieve their objectives. Encourage them to envision the sacrifices required and help them develop a resilient mindset. By fostering a strong commitment, you set the stage for a client who is not easily deterred by challenges.

2. *Risk Mitigation Planning:*

While risks are inherent in any pursuit, work with your clients to develop a comprehensive risk mitigation plan. Help them identify potential obstacles and formulate strategies to navigate these challenges effectively. Emphasize the importance of a proactive approach to risk management, ensuring that they are well-prepared for the uncertainties that may arise during their journey.

3. *Igniting Passion:*

Uncover the passions that drive your clients by delving into their interests, values, and aspirations. Guide them in aligning their goals with their personal passions, transforming their pursuit into a source of intrinsic motivation. Share success stories of individuals who found joy in their endeavors, emphasizing how passion can fuel resilience and perseverance.

Encourage your clients to regularly revisit and reaffirm their commitment, assess and adjust their risk mitigation strategies, and nurture their passion. By integrating these discussions into your coaching sessions, you create a supportive environment that empowers clients to stay on course and weather the storms they may encounter.

Additionally, consider implementing periodic goal assessments and progress evaluations. Celebrate even small victories, reinforcing the positive momentum and instilling a sense of accomplishment. This approach not only boosts your clients' confidence but also strengthens the bond between coach and client, fostering a collaborative relationship focused on shared success.

In essence, your role as a life coach extends beyond providing guidance; it involves sculpting a mindset for success. Through thoughtful conversations, strategic planning, and continuous support, you equip your clients with the tools needed to transform their aspirations into tangible achievements. Witnessing their success becomes a testament to the effectiveness of your coaching, creating a ripple effect that enhances your reputation and attracts more individuals seeking guidance on their path to success.